Frank Ady

Head of Business and Community at Tŷ Hafan

Mel Knight

Group Chief Executive, Castleoak

Our friendship with the wonderful folks at Castleoak knows no bounds which has resulted in this amazing publication. All at Tŷ Hafan hope you have as much fun as we did trying out these super recipes. Thank you again for your continued support, because you care, so can we.

I was delighted in September 2011 when my Foundations Charity Committee colleagues told me that Tŷ Hafan had been selected as our principal charity for two years - although I have to say I was also rather stunned when they told me that their plan was to raise £100,000 in the period!

Since then it has been a thrill to see the tremendous progress they have made towards this ambitious target.

This delightful book typifies the imagination, determination and sheer hard work of my colleagues in supporting such a worthwhile cause and I am most grateful for your support of those efforts through this purchase.

I really hope that the following pages will be very well thumbed and help you to serve up some delicious and memorable food.

Roger Jones

Michelin Star Chef
Vice Chairman & Fellow, The Master Chefs of Great Britain

I have had the privilege to work in the kitchen at Tŷ Hafan and have therefore seen what an important and central part it plays in the support of the hospice children, their families and the wonderful staff and volunteers. A kitchen represents the heart of every home and at Tŷ Hafan, the atmosphere is a warm and welcoming respite away from the families' own homes. It is therefore with great pleasure that I write the foreword to this lovely cookery book illustrated by both Castleoak and Tŷ Hafan children.

I am sure that this book will not only celebrate some great recipes but create some memorable meals and bring some well deserved comfort and enjoyment to everyone involved with Tŷ Hafan and beyond, just like their kitchen does.

Fire Buddy

Johny Keeler Age 9

John Keeler Age 8

To mummy Hope you had a nise day Love JOShua

crany

name Keshar Age 7

HOLLEY 4

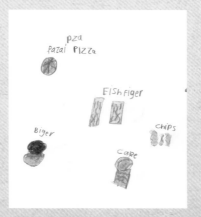

pza
fazal PIZZA

FISH figer

chips

Biger

cake

Johnny Stephens Age 8

Contents

Main meals

Sweet treats and desserts

Aztec Chilli

Main meal

Katie works as an Administrator supporting the rest of the Development Team, enabling them to do what they need to do.

My Auntie gave this Chilli recipe to my mum shortly after she married. My mum has adapted it over the years and more recently added chilli flavoured chocolate to the mix for a slightly unusual twist on the classic Chilli con Carne.

Cooking time:
50 minutes

Makes:
4 servings

What you will need

1 tbsp. olive oil

1 large onion, peeled and chopped

500g (1 lb) lean minced beef

4 cloves of garlic, peeled and chopped

2 400g tins of plum tomatoes

1 400g tin of red kidney beans, drained and rinsed

1 green pepper, de-seeded and chopped

3 tsp. hot chilli powder

½ tsp. salt

3 beef stock cubes, mixed in juice of plum tomatoes

1 large dried red chilli pepper, de-seeded and chopped (optional)

20g (3/4 oz) good quality chilli flavoured dark chocolate, broken into pieces

300g (10½ oz) long-grain rice

Soured cream to serve (optional)

How to make it

1. Gently fry the onions in olive oil until cooked but not browned.

2. Add minced beef and brown, then drain so the mix is dry.

3. Add the other ingredients, except the chilli chocolate. Bring to the boil, then add the chocolate pieces, stir well, turn down the heat, and simmer for 40 minutes.

4. Meanwhile, boil the rice

5. Serve to four hungry people!

Ed Aldridge

Barbecue Chicken

Main meal

Ed works as Head of Development, overseeing the Development Team and ensuring the development process runs smoothly.

This delicious chicken recipe would be great char-grilled over the BBQ on a hot summers day.

Cooking time:
55 minutes

Makes:
4 servings

What you will need

8 chicken joints

1 medium onion, peeled and chopped

5 tbsp. dry cider

5 tbsp. soy sauce

1 tsp. tomato purée

1 garlic clove, crushed

1 tbsp. soft brown sugar

1 tsp. English mustard powder

Few drops olive oil

Freshly milled black pepper

How to make it

1. Pre-heat the oven to 200°C (400°F, Gas Mark 6).

2. Make sure the chicken joints are dry by patting with kitchen roll. Then rub each joint with olive oil and season with freshly milled black pepper.

3. Put the chicken joints in a shallow roasting tin, tucking the chopped onions amongst them and adding a few drops of olive oil. Place the tin on the highest shelf of the oven and cook for 30 minutes.

4. Meanwhile, make up the barbecue sauce by adding the crushed garlic and the rest of the ingredients into a bowl and whisking with a fork until blended thoroughly.

5. When the chicken has cooked for 30 minutes, pour off any excess oil from the roasting tin and pour the barbecue sauce over the chicken. Cook for a further 25 minutes, basting frequently.

Beef in Beer

Main meal

BBC Radio Wales presenter

In Cardiff there was 34 cm of level snow (13 inches) with drifts 8 metres high (26 feet). Wales had just beaten Scotland at rugby 22 points to 14 at the Arms Park and many people were out celebrating including Radio Wales presenter, Roy Noble:

"After the rugby we all dashed off to the nearest hostelry for a beverage or two. It was when we emerged that the shock set in; it was snowing heavily. So heavy, in fact, that many people didn't make it home at all. They had to take refuge in hotels, leisure centres and several convivial houses for days on end.

"Lifelong friendships were made. Fortunately, I got home on the last bus that made it to Aberdare. It was 'touch and go', and such was the camaraderie on the bus, that one fellow from Mountain Ash took his cap off and had a whip-round for the driver.

Villages were cut off for days by huge snow drifts, RAF helicopters air lifted 45 people in South Wales and took food supplies to the more rural areas.

"When I finally struggled home, Elaine had made 'Beef in Beer'. Vic and Margaret, our neighbours, came in, so it became a 'round the warm camp fire' evening."

Cooking time:
2½ hours

Makes:
1 batch

What you will need

900g (2 lb.) chuck steak, cut into 5cm (2") squares

350g (3/4 lb.) onions, peeled, quartered and separated into layers

1 fat garlic clove, crushed

1 tbsp. olive oil

1 sprig of fresh thyme (or ½ tsp. dried)

1 heaped tbsp. plain flour

285ml (10 fl oz) ale

1 bay leaf

Salt and pepper

How to make it

1. Sear the meat in batches in the hot oil until dark brown all over. Remove the meat, add the onions, and brown these before returning the meat to the casserole.

2. Add the flour, reduce the heat and, using a wooden spoon, stir it around to soak up juices.

3. Gradually stir in the ale, slowly bring to a simmer and add the thyme, bay leaf, garlic and seasoning.

4. Cover with a tight fitting lid and do not remove until the end of cooking time.

5. Cook at a gentle simmer for 2½ hours.

Rhydian Roberts

Butternut Squash Soup

Welsh singer, musical theatre performer, TV presenter, and one of the stars of X Factor 2007

I'm not a fan of the British winter and feel the cold, so a warm, healthy soup is ideal as a snack - or as a starter. It goes well with veal steak and roast vegetables.

Cooking time:
30 minutes

Makes:
1 batch

What you will need

1 butternut squash, washed and chopped

1 sweet potato, washed and chopped

1 onion, peeled and chopped

1 small potato, washed and chopped

400 ml (14 fl oz) vegetable stock

Olive oil for roasting

How to make it

1. Place prepared vegetables (with skin left on) in a roasting tray and roast with a drizzle of olive oil for 20 minutes at 200°C (400°F, Gas Mark 6)

2. Allow to cool, then place in a blender with the stock – add a little more stock if the soup is too thick.

3. Transfer to a saucepan and warm through; do not boil.

4. Add salt and pepper to taste.

Andrew Tomlin

Chicken with Cashew Nuts

Main meal

Andrew is the brother of Anne Jenkins, a Foundations Committee member, and Castleoak's Marketing Assistant. Andrew very kindly donated this recipe to us.

Like all good things, there's an element of luck involved. I thought that a good, old traditional Scotch single malt with a smokey tang might add some flavour to a traditional Thai/Chinese recipe - and so it does!

Cooking time:
10-12 minutes

Makes:
2 servings

What you will need

300g (10 ½ oz) chicken breast, thinly sliced

120g (4 oz) deep fried unsalted cashew nuts

3 tbsp. oil

8 cloves of garlic, crushed

2 small onions, peeled and sliced

2 big red chillies, sliced

120 ml (4 fl oz) chicken stock or water

4-8 spring onions, chopped

1 tsp. whisky (preferably a smoked single malt)

2 tbsp. oyster sauce

1 tbsp. soy sauce

1 tbsp. fish sauce

1 tbsp. palm sugar or white sugar

How to make it

1. Heat the oil in a wok and add the garlic.

2. Add the chicken before the garlic browns, along with the onions and chillies.

3. Stirfry for about 3 minutes and add the stock. Stir to combine.

4. Add the mixed sauce ingredients and cashew nuts and stir to combine.

5. Add the spring onions and stir briefly.

6. Add the whisky. Stir in very briefly and remove from the heat.

7. Serve with rice or garlic bread immediately.

Nicola Simic

Chorizo and Prawn Stir fry

Nicola is our Office Caterer. Thanks to her, we're never short of a cuppa when we need one, and are kept well fed at lunchtime!

This simple stir fry is super quick and easy for a mid-week supper or laid back weekend lunch.

Cooking time:
10-15 minutes

Makes:
1 batch

What you will need

1 tbsp. olive oil

1 red pepper, chopped into large chunks

1 yellow pepper, chopped into large chunks

1 chorizo sausage, chopped into chunks

75g (3 oz) cooked white rice per person

Handful of king prawns, peeled and cooked

1 red chilli, chopped

1 tsp. coriander

How to make it

1. In a wok, fry the pepper chunks in the olive oil.

2. Add the chorizo sausage and fry for a further 5 minutes.

3. Add the cooked rice to the wok and warm it through – it will turn orange from the juices of the chorizo.

4. Add the king prawns and chilli, along with the coriander.

5. Fry for a few minutes, serve and enjoy!

Creamy, Cheesy Chicken Curry

Main meal

Nick works as Head of Land Acquisition, overseeing the Land Acquisition Team, and ensuring we have a steady stream of sites coming into our pipeline.

This was something I came up with after a night out when I was feeling hungry and a bit worse for wear! There were no shops open so I had to make do with what I had in the kitchen, and this dish was born!

Cooking time:
30 minutes

Makes:
2-4 servings

What you will need

400g (14 oz) chicken breast, diced

150ml (5 fl oz) beef stock

50g (2 oz) cream cheese

50ml (1 ¾ fl oz) double cream

50g (2 oz) cauliflower, finely grated

1 aubergine, peeled and finely diced

½ courgette, peeled and finely diced

½ medium onion, peeled and finely chopped

2 garlic cloves, peeled and finely chopped

5 tsp. garam masala powder

1 tsp. dried chilli flakes (or 2 fresh chillies, diced)

4 tbsp. vegetable oil

1 tsp. salt

How to make it

1. Heat the oil in a frying pan over a medium heat.

2. Add the aubergine and courgette to the pan and fry for 10 minutes, stirring regularly.

3. Add all the other ingredients except the cream and cream cheese to the pan, stir thoroughly and bring to the boil. Cover and simmer for a further 12 minutes, or until the chicken is cooked.

4. Stir in the cream cheese and double cream and continue cooking until the sauce has reached the desired thickness.

5. Serve with cooked rice, chips, or why not go half 'n' half?

Easy Chicken Paella

Claire is our Corporate Finance Accountant, responsible for keeping our development projects on budget and ensuring our funding is in the right place at the right time.

This recipe was created for my family who aren't seafood lovers but do like paella. If you do like seafood though, I've done this with prawns, scallops and squid and it's fab!

Cooking time:
30 minutes

Makes:
4 servings

What you will need

- 150g (5 oz) chorizo, thinly sliced
- 100g (3 ½ oz) pancetta, diced
- 3 or 4 chicken breasts, diced
- 3 cloves of garlic, finely chopped
- 1 large onion, peeled and finely diced
- 1 red pepper, de-seeded and diced
- 150g (5 oz) mushrooms (optional)
- 2 tsp. thyme flakes
- ½ tsp. dried red chilli flakes
- 570 ml (1 pt) of paella rice
- 2 tsp. paprika
- 150mls (5 fl oz) white wine
- 1 l (2 pt) chicken stock
- 100g (3 ½ oz) frozen peas
- 2 large tomatoes, chopped
- Parsley, lemon wedges, salt and pepper to garnish

How to make it

1. Heat a small amount of olive oil in a paella dish or heavy-based saucepan/casserole dish. Add the chorizo and pancetta and fry until crisp.

2. Add the garlic, onion and pepper and heat until softened. Add the mushrooms if you are using them.

3. Meanwhile, in a separate frying pan, fry the chicken until it's cooked through. If using seafood, add it at this stage. Once cooked, add to the paella.

4. Sprinkle in the thyme, chilli flakes and paella rice and stir until all the grains of rice are coated and glossy. Then add the paprika and white wine and, when bubbling, pour in the hot chicken stock, add the cooked chicken, and cook for 5-10 minutes.

5. Sprinkle in the peas and chopped tomatoes and continue to cook gently for another 10 minutes. It will need fairly regular stirring to stop the rice sticking. If the paella starts to get too dry before the rice is cooked, add a bit more water/stock/wine to loosen. Keep trying the rice to see when it's properly cooked.

6. Once cooked, scatter the chopped parsley over the paella and serve immediately.

7. This is also fab served with a wedge of lemon, some crusty bread or a nice salad.

Easy Lasagne

Chris Czekaj is a Wales international rugby union player, who plays for the Cardiff Blues.

A very simple dish, which tastes great and is always a winner when friends or family come round for dinner.

Cooking time:
1 hour 10 minutes

Makes:
4-6 servings

What you will need

500g (1 lb) lean minced beef

1 white onion, chopped

1 red onion, chopped

1 red pepper, chopped

1 green pepper, chopped

1 large garlic clove, crushed

1 tbsp. olive oil

2 tins chopped tomatoes

1 tbsp. tomato purée

1 packet of dried lasagne sheets

1 packet cheddar cheese sauce mix, made according to packet instructions

1 tsp. dried basil

Any cheese you have in your fridge, grated

Salt and pepper to taste

How to make it

1. Preheat oven to 180°C (350°F, Gas Mark 4)

2. In a large, non-stick saucepan, heat the oil over a high temperature and brown the beef, stirring and breaking it up as you go. Once browned, add the onion, garlic and peppers and fry for a further 2-3 minutes.

3. Add the tinned tomatoes, tomato purée, dried basil, salt and pepper, stir well and once it has come to the boil turn the heat right down and simmer for 20 minutes, or until the liquid has evaporated.

4. In a large, rectangular, oven-proof dish, begin to assemble the lasagne by firstly spreading a third of the beef mixture across the bottom of the dish, then a layer of lasagne sheets. Repeat this process twice.

5. Top with the cheese sauce and a layer of grated cheese to finish.

6. Bake in the centre of the oven for 30 minutes, or until it is cooked through (test by inserting a knife into the centre and checking that the knife comes out piping hot).

7. Serve immediately with steamed vegetables and garlic bread.

21

Andrew Duggan

Fish Pie

Andrew is Castleoak's HR Manager, who also serves as a Foundations Committee member.

This recipe is a Duggan family favourite. It's really simple to make and tastes fantastic. It's great straight out of the oven or makes a meal in a minute if you freeze and re-heat at a later date. My five year old daughter and 18 month old son love it. Just remember it's too nice just for kids - save yourself a portion too!

Cooking time:
1 hour

Makes:
6 servings

What you will need

1 kg (2lb) potatoes, peeled

Knob of butter

750g (1½lb) fish, boned and cut into 1cm chunks

4 large carrots, peeled and grated

Grated rind and juice of 1 lemon

200g (7oz) cheddar cheese, grated

2 tbsp. olive oil

Salt and pepper to taste

How to make it

1. Boil the potatoes. When soft, mash with butter and set aside.

2. Into a large dish, add the carrots, cheese, lemon rind, lemon juice, olive oil, salt and pepper. Mix well.

3. Spoon in the mashed potato and spread evenly across the top to a depth of roughly 1-2 cm.

4. Place in the middle of a pre-heated oven at 200°C (400°F, Gas Mark 6) and cook for 40 minutes, or until the top has browned.

5. Serve with vegetables or baked beans.

Fisherman's Chicken

Dame Shirley Bassey, DBE is a Welsh singer. She found fame in the mid-1950s and has been called "one of the most popular female vocalists in Britain during the last half of the 20th century". Shirley was born in Tiger Bay, Cardiff (now known as Cardiff Bay).

Cooking time:
45 minutes

Makes:
2-4 servings

What you will need

2-4 chicken breasts

1-2 tins of good quality lobster bisque

1 medium tin of sliced mushrooms (or 4 fresh mushrooms, thinly sliced)

1 large brown onion, coarsely chopped

Butter

Brandy

100g (3 ½ oz) packet of frozen small shrimps, peeled

How to make it

1. Sweat the onion in a frying pan until golden. Remove from the heat and strain – repeat process to brown the mushrooms. Leave both to cool and then refrigerate.

2. Place the chicken breasts in a casserole dish with a little butter and cover with the lobster bisque. Cook in the oven at 180°C (350°F, Gas Mark 4) for about 30 minutes, or until the chicken is cooked through. When done allow to cool before refrigerating overnight.

3. When ready to serve, remove the chicken breasts from the marinade and reheat the liquid in a saucepan over a gentle heat to reduce it a little. Add the cooked chicken breasts to the pan and reheat gently.

4. Five minutes before serving, add the mushrooms, onion, peeled shrimp and a good splash of brandy.

5. Mix gently together to warm through and serve with plain boiled rice.

25

Gadge's Gut Buster

Gadge works for Castleoak as a Customer Care Operative.

This was my Granny's favourite recipe!

Cooking time:
20-30 minutes

Makes:
1 gut buster

What you will need

680g (1 ½ lb) lean minced beef

1 large Spanish onion, peeled and sliced

3 or 4 beef stock cubes

Salt and pepper to taste

1 tbsp. vegetable/sunflower oil

How to make it

1. Fry the onion in oil until browned.

2. Add the mince and stock cubes and cook for 20-25 minutes.

3. Season to taste.

4. Serve with Welsh buttered crusty bread and a bottle of Bollinger 75 (a very good year!)

5. For pudding, I like mini apple pies covered in custard and heated in the microwave!

Ian Garland

Hunter's Lamb

Ian works as a Commercial Surveyor for Castlecoak.

A sort of Italian dish for that winter's evening, we adapted it from an Italian cook book that we use and played around with the ingredients to get it to our taste (or more to mine as my wife's vegetarian!). A regular dish that is eaten at home, a bit like a stew but without all the lumpy bits in it.

Cooking time:
25 minutes

Makes:
2 servings

What you will need

6 slices of parma ham

2 sprigs of fresh rosemary

2 lamb neck fillets

1½ - 2 tbsp. extra virgin olive oil

1½ celery sticks, roughly chopped

2 cloves of garlic, peeled and thinly sliced

1 carrot, peeled and roughly chopped

½ - ¾ shallot, roughly chopped

½ a red chilli pepper, chopped

60ml (2 fl oz) red wine

225ml (8 fl oz) meat stock

½ tsp. flour, mixed to a paste with some butter

Salt and black pepper to taste

How to make it

1. Preheat the oven to 220°C (425°F, Gas Mark 7)

2. Lay the parma ham on a board in two stacks. Place a sprig of rosemary on each stack.

3. Remove any fat from the lamb, season with salt and pepper, and place a fillet on each stack. Tightly roll the parma ham around the meat to form parcels and secure with a cocktail stick pierced through the meat.

4. Heat the oil in a pan, add the vegetables, garlic and chilli and sauté for about 5 minutes, stirring regularly. Place to one side.

5. Cook the meat parcels over a high heat, seam-side down first, for about 2 minutes, turning regularly until browned all over.

6. Pour the wine over the meat, bring to the boil, and simmer for about 2 minutes. Add the stock and bring back to the boil. Cover with a lid and transfer to the oven for 12-15 minutes, or until the lamb is tender but still pink in the centre. When done, remove the lamb from the pan and leave to rest, whilst keeping it warm.

7. Empty the remaining contents of the pan into a food processor, blend until smooth, then sieve back into the pan and place over a low heat. Whisk in the flour-and-butter paste, a little at a time, until the sauce is thickened to your liking, then re-add the lamb parcels.

8. Spoon a little of the sauce over the lamb and leave for about a minute before serving with warm gnocchi and some warm olive bread.

Lancashire Meat and Potato Pie

Main meal

Vicki is Castlecook's HR Assistant. Vicki worked on the cookbook editorial team, helping to bring it to life!

As you can imagine, this is quite a hearty meal. My mum always used to make this meal on a Friday or Saturday night when I was a teenager. It was usually the night I was going to the local discotheque for a night out. She swears blind it wasn't to soak up the copious amounts of alcohol I consumed, but I think differently!

Cooking time:
1 ½ hours

Makes:
1 large pie

What you will need

700g (1 ½ lb.) King Edward potatoes, peeled and cubed

2 carrots, peeled and chopped

1 onion, peeled and chopped

Beef dripping

1 packet of Suet dumpling mix

450g (1 lb.) steak and kidney pieces

50g (2 oz) flour

How to make it

1. Place half the potatoes and the carrots in a large casserole dish.

2. Add a layer of the steak and kidney pieces and onion, and sprinkle with flour.

3. Top with the rest of the potatoes and add enough water to just cover the contents of the casserole dish.

4. Cook for approximately 45 minutes at 200°C (400°F/Gas mark 6).

5. Make up the suet according to the packet instructions, roll out and place on top of the casserole dish

6. Cook for another 45 minutes, or until the crust is light brown.

7. Serve with red cabbage or beetroot.

Mac 'n' Cheese

Jonathan Pryce, CBE is a Welsh stage and film actor. He has participated in big-budget films such as Evita, Tomorrow Never Dies, Pirates of the Caribbean and The New World. His career in theatre has also been prolific, and he has won two Tony Awards.

Jonathan's son, Gabriel, co-owns Rita's Bar & Dining in London and this is one of their signature dishes.

Cooking time:
30-35 minutes

Makes:
1 batch

What you will need

500g (18 oz) macaroni	5 green chillies, sliced into coins
100g (3 ½ oz) salted butter	1 lime
150g (5 oz) plain flour	2 avocados
250g (9 oz) Gruyere cheese, grated	1 bunch of fresh coriander
150g (5 oz) Red Leicester cheese, grated	Salt
	Black pepper
500ml (1 pt) full fat milk	White pepper
2 tsp English mustard powder	

How to make it

1. Boil a pan of heavily salted water and add the macaroni, cooking until tender. Drain and transfer pasta to a baking dish.

2. Make a basic roux by slowly melting the butter. Then add the flour, followed by the mustard powder.

3. After about five minutes, slowly add the milk and cook until the sauce has the consistency of pouring cream.

4. Add the grated cheeses, a handful at a time, until the sauce is smooth and all the cheese is melted.

5. Add the chillies.

6. Pour the sauce over the macaroni and stir through, so everything is coated with a bit of sauce and all the chillies are evenly dispersed. Add a few grinds of black pepper, and salt to taste. Place in a hot oven for 10 to 15 minutes.

7. While the mac is in the oven, mash the flesh of the avocados with the juice of the limes, and salt and white pepper to taste to make a very basic guacamole.

8. Remove the mac from the oven and place under a grill to brown and crisp the top. Serve each portion with a small dollop of avocado sauce and a sprinkle of chopped coriander.

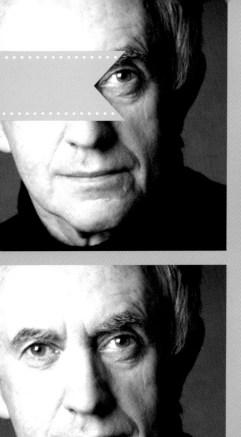

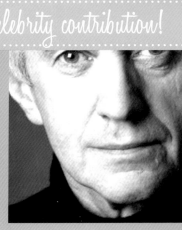

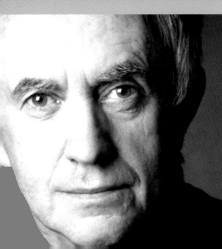

Steve Bucknell

Penne all' Arrabbiata

Steve is Managing Director of Castleoak's Development division, responsible for overseeing the Development, Planning, and Land Acquisition Teams.

I like spicy food and I like pasta. This dish combines the two, and is quick, simple and delicious!

Cooking time:
30 minutes

Makes:
2 servings

What you will need

6 rashers smoked streaky bacon, cut into lardons

1 large onion, peeled and diced

As many garlic cloves as desired, crushed

1 400g tin of chopped tomatoes

2 tbsp. tomato purée

1 vegetable stock cube

As many chillies as you desire, chopped

3 or 4 stems of fresh basil, or 3-4 tsp. dried

2 tbsp. olive oil

200g (7 oz) penne pasta, fresh or dried

½ a jar of pesto sauce

Parmesan for garnish, grated

Red wine of choice (optional)

How to make it

1. Sauté the onions, bacon and chillies in olive oil over a medium heat.

2. When the onions are soft, add the garlic.

3. Before the garlic burns, add the tomatoes, purée and stock.

4. Bring to the boil and add the basil – leave to simmer.

5. If you want to enrich the sauce, add a dash of the red wine.

6. Meanwhile, bring a pan of salted water to the boil and cook your pasta according to the instructions on the packet.

7. When the pasta is al dente (firm to the bite), strain it, throw in the pesto sauce, and toss it around until well coated.

8. Put the pasta on a serving dish or plate, pour the sauce over, and garnish with grated parmesan according to taste.

Stephen Williams

Pork Medallions in Mustard and Cider Sauce

Stephen works in our Procurement Team as one of our Buyers.

Almost every Friday night for over 20 years, our meal of choice was an Indian take-away. About 18 months ago, our favourite restaurant changed their chef and the meal we had was awful. I was so upset that I bravely announced that from now on I would cook our Friday evening meal! My history of cooking was a lasagne made once a year at Christmas for the family get together, so this outburst was a little ambitious.

Nevertheless, I stuck to my guns and the following Friday we had a nice simple chicken dish. I now do most of the cooking at home and I really do enjoy it. This recipe is probably my default or signature dish. The quantities are approximate and can be adjusted to suit your own taste or appetite.

Cooking time:
30 minutes

Makes:
2 servings

What you will need

1 pork tenderloin, cut into 2cm (3/4") pieces

1 tbsp. dried apricots, diced

1 tbsp. sultanas, diced

1 tbsp. wholegrain mustard

180ml (6 fl oz) double cream

75ml (2 ½ fl oz) cider

200g (7 oz) potatoes, washed, dried and cubed, skin on

2 sprigs of rosemary, chopped

2 cloves of garlic, crushed

2 carrots, washed, peeled and cut into batons

50g (2 oz) green beans, cut to the same length as the carrots

How to make it

1. Preheat the oven to 200°C (400°F, Gas Mark 6)

2. Put 2 tbsp. olive oil on a flat baking tray and place in the oven for a few minutes. Remove the tray and place on the hob on a medium flame to maintain the temperature.

3. Put the dried potato cubes onto the tray and coat all over with the oil, add the rosemary, and place in the oven. After 10 minutes, remove the tray, turn the cubes, add the garlic and cook for a further 15 minutes, or until golden brown and crisp. Remove and season to taste.

4. Meanwhile, prepare the green beans and cook with the carrot in boiling salted water for 20 minutes (less if you prefer firmer vegetables).

5. While the potatoes and vegetables are cooking, season both sides of the pork medallions and fry on a medium heat in a little olive oil for 2 minutes on each side. Remove from the pan to rest.

6. Add the cider to the pan and heat for 1 minute. Reduce the heat then add the apricots, sultanas, mustard and double cream. Bring to the boil then return the meat to the pan, mix thoroughly and reduce for 1 minute.

7. Garnish the green beans and carrots with a knob of butter and some black pepper, and serve with the potatoes and pork.

Royal Rumble's Homemade Pizza

Main meal

Nic works as a Property and Asset Manager, responsible for carrying out site inspections and overseeing the management of our leased developments.

This is much easier to make and prepare than you think and makes a fantastic alternative to buying/ordering ready-made pizza. It's well worth a little bit of effort and you'll be amazed at how flavoursome and fun this is to make! The dough can be made the day before if covered in cling flim and kept in the fridge, and the choice of topping is endless!

Cooking time:
10-15 minutes

Makes:
3-4 medium pizzas

What you will need

325-350 ml (11-12 fl oz) lukewarm water

1 tbsp. active dried yeast (or 1 x 75g sachet)

550g (19 ½ oz) strong white bread flour

1 tsp. salt

½ tsp. ground black pepper

2 tsp. clear honey or sugar

2 tbsp. extra virgin olive oil

Dry polenta/semolina for dusting (optional)

1 jar of ready-made pizza topping or pasta sauce

1 red pepper, de-seeded and sliced

1 artichoke, sliced

Handful of pitted black olives

6-8 slices of parma ham, torn into shreds

Handful of capers and anchovies

Handful of mushrooms, sliced

Mozzarella or cheddar, grated

How to make it

1. Pour 325 (11 fl oz) of water into a bowl and mix in the dried yeast, honey/sugar and olive oil. Stir until dissolved (add a little more water if necessary) and leave to rest in a warm place for ten minutes for the yeast to activate (a thin layer of bubbles will begin to form on top of the mix).

2. Sieve the flour, salt and pepper into a large bowl. Make a well in the middle and slowly pour the yeast mixture into the well, while mixing with a fork. Keep adding liquid until the mixture forms a soft and slightly sticky dough.

3. Transfer the dough to a flour-dusted surface and knead until it's smooth, springy and pliable. Place in a large, lightly oiled or dusted bowl and cover with clingfilm. Leave in a warm place for about 1 hour until it's doubled in size.

4. Remove the clingfilm and push the air out of the dough. Divide into 3 or 4 equal round balls and either use or cover and refrigerate for later.

5. Sprinkle a work surface with polenta (or flour). Flatten/stretch each ball of dough with a rolling pin (or your hands) until you've reached your desired size.

6. Lightly oil a pizza tray/baking sheet and sprinkle with polenta/flour before transferring the pizza base(s) onto it. Leave to rest for 5-10 minutes before covering each base with the pizza topping/pasta sauce, then your topping ingredients, and finally the grated cheese.

7. Cook in a preheated oven at 220°C (425°F, Gas Mark 7) for 10-15 minutes until the crust is golden brown.

Sausage Sizzler in a Bun

Simple cooking. Our favourite pastime at the hospice, with this recipe being an all-time fave!

Cooking time:
20 minutes

Makes:
15 burgers

What you will need

- 2kg (4 ½ lb) sausage meat
- 3 onions, finely chopped
- 1 tsp. mixed herbs
- 2 eating apples, finely chopped
- 2x 410g tins baked beans, drained and puréed
- 2 tsp. salt and pepper, plus extra to taste
- 2 tbsp. tomato purée

- 2 cloves garlic
- 2 carrots, finely chopped
- 2 sticks of celery
- 1 x 800g tin of tomato Passata
- 1 tsp. sugar
- Vegetable oil
- Burger buns

How to make it

1. Fry two of the onions in the vegetable oil until soft.
2. Add the mixed herbs and the apples and cook for a few more minutes until the apple is soft.
3. Remove from the heat and add the sausage meat, baked beans, salt, pepper and tomato purée and mix together.
4. Mould into burgers with seasoned flour and fry for 10-15 minutes until cooked through.
5. Meanwhile, place the remaining onion, garlic, carrots, celery and Passata in a pan and cook until really soft.
6. Add salt, pepper and sugar to taste. Purée into a tomato sauce.
7. Serve the burgers in buns with the tomato sauce and some grated cheese or a fried egg.

Cath Smith

Simple Steak Burgers & Wedges

Cath works as a Research Analyst, helping to determine the suitability of sites as potential care home locations. Cath is also a Foundations Committee member and, along with the rest of the cookbook editorial team, worked to bring this book into your kitchen!

Both the burgers and the wedges came about when we were fed up of using pre-bought reconstituted or frozen varieties, and I decided to see how easy it would be to make them myself. The wedges have become a staple in our house and the burgers are quicker to make than rummaging in the freezer or popping to the shops!

Cooking time:
30 minutes

Makes:
2 servings

What you will need

500g (1 lb) good quality steak mince

Pinch of black pepper

2 large garlic cloves, crushed

4 tbsp. olive oil

1-2 tsp. dried crushed chilli flakes

1 small onion, peeled and finely chopped

Dash of tabasco sauce

2 burger buns/crusty rolls/ciabattas according to taste

1 tbsp. Cajun seasoning

4-6 large Desiree potatoes, cut into wedges, skin on

How to make it

1. Heat a large saucepan of water until boiling – add the potatoes and allow to simmer for around 10 minutes, or until they're soft enough for a fork to go through easily without being so soft that they fall apart.

2. While the potatoes are boiling, in a baking tray or roasting tin, mix 2 tbsp. olive oil with the Cajun seasoning until you're left with a paste.

3. Drain the potatoes and combine with the marinade in the tray – turn them over until they're well coated and spread out in the tray.

4. Cook in a pre-heated oven at around 220°C (425°F, Gas Mark 7) for around 20 minutes, or until golden brown and crispy.

5. Meanwhile, put the steak mince, the rest of the olive oil, black pepper, garlic, onion, chilli flakes and tabasco sauce into a bowl and mix together with a fork or your hands. This should take roughly a minute.

6. Squish roughly half the mixture into a burger shape with your hands and place on a grill pan – repeat for the other half.

7. Grill for 15-20 minutes and serve in the buns/rolls with the wedges and, if you wish, salad.

Mark Collins

Sophie's Mild Thai Red Curry

Main meal

Mark works as our IT Support Technician and is always on hand to help out in times of computer-related crisis.

We sometimes make this on a Saturday night as a change from the regular Saturday night takeaway. Sophie (my 9 year old daughter) likes it as it's a delicious, mild curry, but I like to spice mine up a bit by sprinkling a few sliced birdseye chillies on top!

Cooking time:
30-35 minutes

Makes:
4 servings

What you will need

- 1 tsp. vegetable oil
- 4 chicken breasts
- 1 large onion, thinly sliced into rings
- 2 garlic cloves, crushed
- 2 red peppers, de-seeded and cut into chunks
- 8 baby sweetcorn, halved lengthways (optional)
- 1 stalk of fresh lemon grass, bashed with a rolling pin
- 2 tsp. fresh ginger, grated
- 400ml (2 ½ oz) coconut milk
- 150ml (5 fl oz) chicken stock
- 2 tbsp. Thai red curry paste
- 1 tbsp. fish sauce
- 2 tbsp. fresh coriander, chopped, plus extra to garnish

How to make it

1. Heat the oil in a pan, add the garlic and seal the chicken for 4/5 minutes over a medium heat.

2. Add the onion and cook for a further 2 minutes.

3. Add the peppers, baby sweetcorn, lemon grass, ginger, coconut milk, stock and red curry paste. Stir in the fish sauce and coriander.

4. Bring to the boil and then leave to simmer over a low heat for 20-25 minutes, stirring occasionally.

5. Remove the lemongrass before serving.

6. Sprinkle with chopped coriander

7. Serve with rice or chips, according to preference.

Dean Richards

Spanish Chicken

Dean works as one of our Contracts Managers, and is also a Foundations Committee member.

This recipe was first introduced to me by my sister-in-law, and now my wife Donna has taken it on as a successful dish in the Richards household.

Cooking time:
1 hour

Makes:
4 servings

What you will need

4 chicken thighs

1-2 chorizo sausages, sliced

A dozen small potatoes, washed and quartered

2 red onions, peeled and quartered

2 tbsp. olive oil

1 tsp. dried oregano

Pinch of salt

Zest of 1 orange, grated

How to make it

1. Place the chicken thighs on a baking sheet.

2. Add the chorizo, red onions and potatoes.

3. Toss in the olive oil, and sprinkle with salt, oregano and orange zest.

4. Bake in a pre-heated oven at 200°C (400°F, Gas Mark 6) for at least an hour.

5. Serve with salad leaves, dressing and olive bread (optional).

Geraint Thomas MBE

Born and bred in Cardiff, South Wales, Geraint Thomas, MBE, is a professional cyclist. Riding on the road for Team Sky, Geraint is also track cycling World Champion and boasts two Olympic Gold medals.

My favourite style of cooking is easy, and this is a great recipe for just that. I love to BBQ and look for any excuse, I even had a BBQ on New Year's Eve once. This spiced Welsh Beef steak is fantastic because you get fantastic flavour from the meat and that extra sensation from the spices. While my diet can be restricted when I'm racing, there's nothing I like better than a nice Welsh Beef steak when I get the chance to relax.

Cooking time:
20-25 minutes

Makes:
2 servings

What you will need

2 Welsh Beef rib eye steaks (could use sirloin/ rump)

½ tsp. cumin seeds

½ tsp. dried cumin

½ tsp. coriander seeds

½ tsp. dried coriander

½ tsp. dried chilli flakes

1 clove garlic

Seasoning

1 tbsp. oil

1 small onion, peeled and cut into chunks

1 eating apple, peeled, cored and thickly sliced

1 small red pepper, deseeded and thickly sliced

1 400g (14 oz) tin pineapple rings in natural ju

2 gherkins, chopped and 1 tbsp. vinegar from j

1 tbsp. brown ketchup/sauce

2 tbsp. tomato ketchup

How to make it

1. Place all spices, garlic and seasoning in a pestle and mortar (or use a small dish and wooden spoon or rolling pin) and lightly 'pound' together to break down spice seeds and garlic.

2. Place steaks in a shallow dish, sprinkle over the spice mixture and rub into the steaks to cover and coat.

3. Leave covered until ready to cook.

4. Make BBQ sauce – place oil, onion, apple and pepper in a pan and lightly cook together for 1-2 minutes.

5. Add all remaining ingredients, bring to the boil and then simmer for about 15 minutes until the vegetables have softened slightly.

6. Cook steaks on a hot preheated BBQ, grill or griddle for about 3 minutes each side for rare, 4 minutes each side for medium.

7. Serve steaks with the chunky rustic BBQ sauce, mixed green salad and chunky potato wedges.

Main meal

Celebrity contribution!

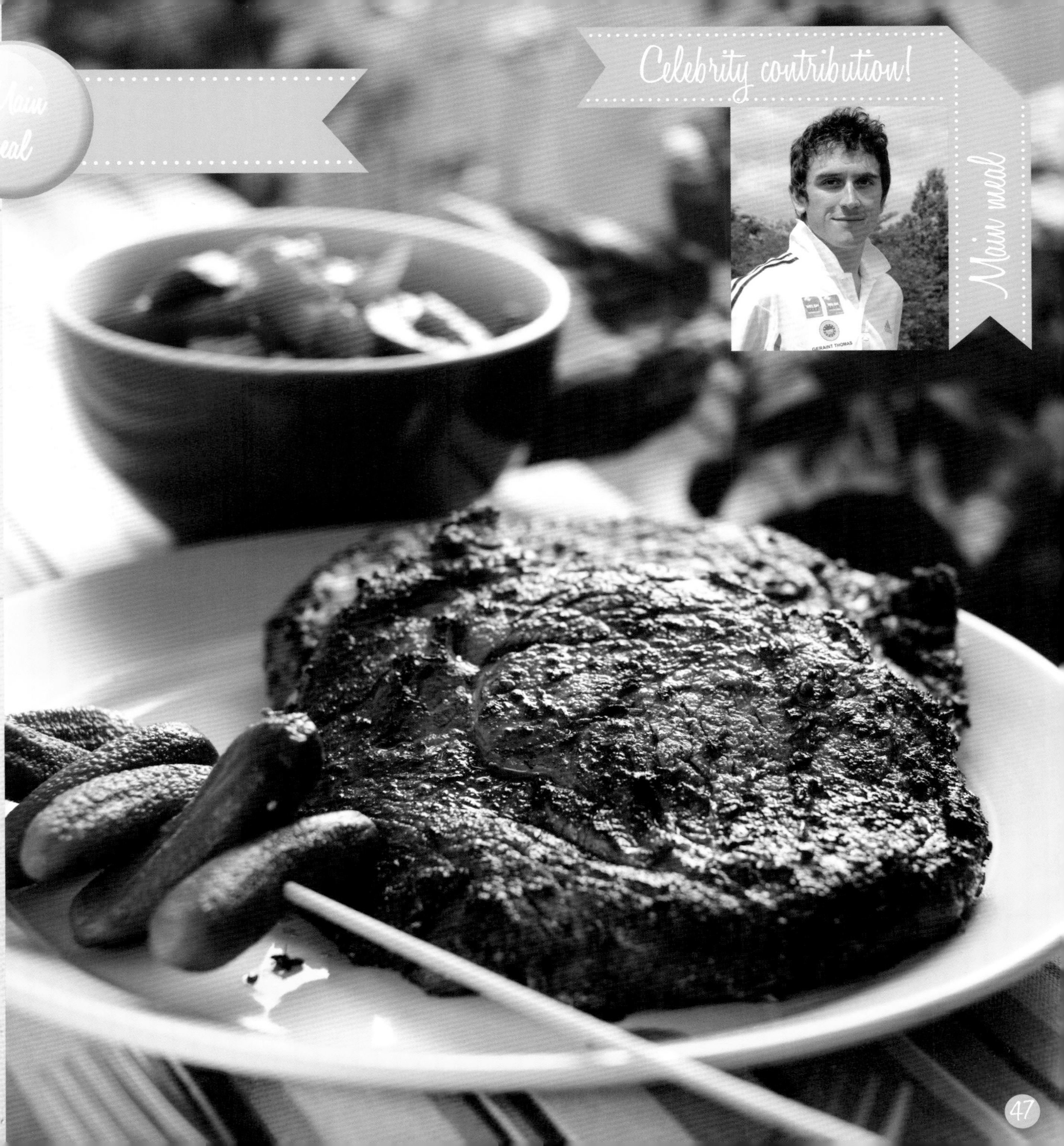

Main meal

Ceri Booth

Tasty Salmon Bake

Ceri works part-time for our Communications and Marketing Department on a freelance basis and has her own company, The Creative Booth (www.thecreativebooth.com).

This dish is a firm favourite of mine. With so few ingredients it's easy to remember and makes a healthy salmon meal all the more tasty and satisfying. The melted cheese on top is a real treat - and I always sprinkle on an extra handful for good measure. If you don't mind the calories, you can also stir in an extra dollop of crème fraiche.

Cooking time:
40 minutes

Makes:
4 servings

What you will need

4 fresh salmon fillets (or equivalent tinned)

A dozen or so new potatoes

200g (7 oz) peas

50g (2 oz) cheese, grated

200g (7 oz) tub of crème fraiche

How to make it

1. If using fresh salmon, season according to your liking (eg. with herbs, lemon juice and a little butter), wrap in foil and cook in a pre-heated oven at 200°C (400°F, Gas Mark 6) for around 25 minutes, or until it flakes with a fork.

2. Cook the peas until tender.

3. Slice the new potatoes lengthways into slim discs – you should be able to get around four slices per potato – and boil for 10 minutes.

4. Combine the flaked salmon and peas in an oven-proof dish with the crème fraiche

5. Place the potato slices on top of the salmon and peas, forming a double layer if needed.

6. Sprinkle the grated cheese on top of the potato.

7. Place under a medium-high grill until the cheese is golden brown.

8. Serve with fresh green beans and broccoli.

Brad Fisher

Ultimate Man Dinner

Brad is a Construction Manager, responsible for overseeing the construction of our care homes.

This light snack will go down well for some of us and make a good meal for anyone else!

Cooking time:
10-15 minutes

Makes:
1 ultimate man dinner

What you will need

1 round loaf of crusty Italian bread

2 ribeye steaks

1 large onion, peeled and chopped

450g (1 lb) mushrooms, sliced

1 pack of bacon rashers

1 block of Swiss cheese, sliced

1 bottle of Worcestershire sauce

1 jar of mayonnaise

1 jar of Dijon mustard

How to make it

1. Cut the top off the loaf and hollow out the bread, keeping the top for later.

2. In separate pans, fry the steaks, mushrooms, onions and bacon – try to leave the steaks a little rare (pink inside) as they will continue cooking whilst in the sandwich.

3. Place one of the steaks inside the hollowed out loaf and cover with sauce – I like to adopt a 'half n half' approach so cover one half with a thick layer of Worcestershire sauce and the other with Dijon mustard and mayonnaise.

4. Add a layer of bacon, then a layer of Swiss cheese, then spoon in as many mushrooms and onions as will fit.

5. Add the other steak, along with the juices from the pan they were cooked in.

6. Add a little more Worcestershire sauce/Dijon mustard/mayonnaise and another layer of Swiss cheese.

7. Put the lid back on the loaf, wrap in butcher's paper and then tin foil.

8. Place a heavy cutting board on top of the loaf, along with any dumb bell weights you have to hand, and wait for approximately 4 hours.

9. Remove the weights, unwrap the sandwich and enjoy!

STEFFAN

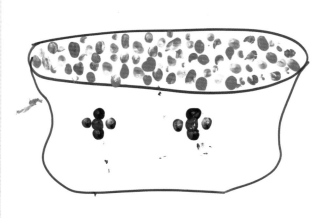

Elliot

PIZZA

AGE: 7

NAME: KESHNI

To mummy Hope You had a nise day Love Joshua

CHELSEA 5yrs

Turn over for sweet treats and desserts...

Sandra Smith

Andrea's Marshmallow Cheesecake

Dessert

Sandra is the mum-in-law of Cath Smith, Research Analyst for Castleoak.

Sandra very kindly donated this recipe which belonged to her friend, Andrea, who sadly passed away with cancer when she was 53.

Preparation:
2 hours +

Makes:
10-12 servings

What you will need

- 285ml (10 fl oz) double cream
- 225g (8 oz) cream cheese
- 225g (8 oz) marshmallows
- 120ml (4 fl oz) milk
- 170g (6 oz) biscuits, crushed
- 85g (3 oz) butter, melted

How to make it

1. Mix the melted butter with the biscuits and press into a flan dish to form the base of the cheesecake. Chill in the fridge until set.

2. Dissolve the marshmallows in the milk by heating very gently over a low heat and stirring constantly.

3. Soften the cheese and beat in the cream.

4. Mix the ingredients together and pour over the cheesecake base.

5. Put in the fridge to set. A couple of hours should be enough but longer is better.

Lynda Davies

Apricot and Pecan Cookies

Sweet treat

Lynda is Castleoak's Receptionist; and the first friendly face people see when they come to visit our office.

This is my mum's best friend's recipe. These deliciously simple, nutty cookies taste great with a hot cup of tea.

Cooking time:
10-12 minutes

Makes:
1 batch (approx 20 cookies)

What you will need

225g (8 oz) butter, softened

140g (5 oz) caster sugar

1 egg yolk, lightly beaten

2 tsp. vanilla extract

280g (10 oz) plain flour

Grated rind of 1 orange

50g (2 oz) ready-to-eat dried apricots, chopped

100g (3 ½ oz) pecan nuts, finely chopped

How to make it

1. Put the butter and sugar into a mixing bowl and mix well with a wooden spoon.

2. Beat in the egg yolk and vanilla extract.

3. Sift together the flour and a pinch of salt into the mixture, add the orange rind and apricots and stir until thoroughly combined.

4. Shape the dough into a log. Spread the pecans in the bottom of a shallow tray and roll the log in the nuts until well coated. Wrap in clingfilm and chill in the fridge for 30-60 minutes.

5. Pre-heat the oven to 190°C (375°F, Gas Mark 5). Line two baking sheets with baking parchment.

6. Unwrap the dough and cut into 0.5cm (1/4") slices with a sharp knife. Spread the slices out on the prepared baking sheets so they're well apart.

7. Bake for 10-12 minutes. Leave to cool on the baking sheets for 5-10 minutes, then using a palette knife or spatula, carefully transfer to a wire rack to cool completely.

Banoffee Pie

Mel is our Group Chief Executive, and we love that he's taken time out from running the company to contribute a recipe!

Banoffee Pie has become a firm family favourite over the years. My wife Mandy makes one for most family parties, and it is always the first dessert to disappear. It last appeared at our daughter Rachel's 21st birthday party in June. Enjoy!

Cooking time:
30 minutes

Makes:
10 servings

What you will need

300g (10 ½ oz) unsalted butter

275g (10 oz) plain or chocolate digestives, crushed

175g (6 oz) caster sugar

1 400g (14 oz) can of sweetened, condensed milk

300ml (10 ½ fl oz) double cream, whipped

2 ripe bananas, peeled and sliced

1 milk chocolate bar, grated

How to make it

1. Make the base first by melting 125g (4 ½ oz) of the butter in a saucepan and adding the crushed digestives. Mix well and transfer to a flan dish, pressing into the bottom and sides of the dish. Chill until firm (about 20 minutes).

2. Combine the rest of the butter and sugar in a non-stick pan. Stir over a low heat until the butter has melted and the sugar has dissolved.

3. Add the condensed milk and stir continuously over a low heat until the mixture starts to bubble. Continue stirring for a few minutes until the mixture thickens (3-4 minutes).

4. Pour the mixture into the flan dish and chill until set.

5. Arrange the bananas over the caramel filling and top with whipped cream. Decorate with the grated chocolate and serve!

Sam Tabiner

Blackbirds

Sweet treat

Sam works for Castleoak as Sales Support Manager, helping to secure new sales and foster new relationships with potential clients.

Had something down at my mum's that reminded me of my youth! Reminds me of camping with the scouts and BBQs in the back garden. We used to have them every year on Fireworks night! Good for getting the calories in when you're marathon training!!

Cooking time:
5-10 minutes

Makes:
1 sandwich

What you will need

2 slices of slightly stale white bread

Knob of butter

1 tbsp. blackberry jam

1 packet of pancake batter mix, made up according to packet instructions

50g (2 oz) white sugar

Strawberries and cream for garnish (optional)

How to make it

1. Butter both slices of bread, spread each slice with blackberry jam, and make a sandwich out of them with the jam on the inside.

2. Cut the crusts off and cut into quarters.

3. Dip the quarters into the made up pancake batter.

4. Place in a frying pan and fry in butter until crisp and golden.

5. Coat in white sugar.

6. Add cream and strawberries if you wish.

7. Carefully eat while still hot!

Callum Bassett-Jones

Brownies

Castleoak work experience Intern

Callum spent a week at Castloak on work experience while we were in the process of putting this book together. He enjoyed his time with us so much, he brought a batch of his mum's brownies in for us all on his last day (which went down *very* well in the office!), and very kindly donated the recipe to us too!

Cooking time:
25-30 minutes

Makes:
15 - 20 brownies

What you will need

200g (7 oz) unsalted butter

100g (3 ½ oz) dark chocolate

350g (12 oz) light soft brown sugar

4 large eggs

1 tsp. vanilla extract

200g (7 oz) self-raising flour, sifted

Pinch of salt

200g Toblerone bar, finely cut

How to make it

1. Preheat the oven to 180°C (350°F, Gas Mark 4).

2. Brush a 28cmx18cm (11x7") baking tin with a little melted butter, and line with greaseproof paper.

3. Melt the butter and chocolate in a heatproof bowl suspended over a saucepan of barely simmering water. Remove from the heat and add the sugar.

4. Beat the eggs and the vanilla extract together and add to the chocolate mixture.

5. Stir the sifted flour and salt into the mixture, before adding the Toblerone.

6. Bake for 25-30 minutes until the top is crispy and the inside is soft.

7. Leave to cool in the tin before cutting into squares.

Bryn Terfel

Chocolate Bits

 Sweet treat

Welsh bass-baritone and founder of the Faenol Festival.

Bryn's mum's recipe - a favourite from when he was a boy.

Cooking time:
20-30 minutes

Makes:
1 batch

What you will need

50g (2 oz) margarine

100g (3 ½ oz) desiccated coconut

100g (3 ½ oz) caster sugar

50g (2 oz) cherries, washed, dried and chopped

1 egg, beaten

Large bar of your preferred chocolate

How to make it

1. Line a swiss roll tin with cooking foil or greaseproof paper.

2. Melt the chocolate and spread in the tin; leave to set.

3. Melt the margarine slowly, before stirring in the dry ingredients and cherries.

4. Add the beaten egg last, mix well, and spread this over the set chocolate.

5. Bake in a preheated oven at 175°C (350°F, Gas Mark 4) for 20-30 minutes, or until brown.

6. Leave to cool, then cut into squares of your own choice.

Margaret Knight

Fruit Cake

Sweet treat

Margaret is the very proud mum of Colwyn, our Construction Director, and our Group Chief Executive, Mel. Colwyn very kindly donated this recipe on their mum's behalf.

When I was younger, I remember my mother cooking fruit cake regularly in the family cottage. On occasions, she would bake an extra large cake to share with my three uncles, Jack, Harry and Arthur, who all lived in the village. She never used a recipe, but always knew exactly which ingredients to use. It was always delicious. Good cooking was always part of village life and has since run in the family. I am sure that this has given my wonderful sons a good start in life and contributed to Colwyn and Melville's success.

Cooking time:
2-2 ¼ hours

Makes:
20cm (8") cake

What you will need

250g (9 oz) soft margarine

250g (9 oz) light muscovado sugar

4 eggs

250g (9 oz) self-raising flour

250g (9 oz) raisins

250g (9 oz) sultanas

125g (4 ½ oz) glace cherry halves

½ tsp. ground mixed spice

1 tbsp. brandy

How to make it

1. Lightly grease a deep 20cm (8") cake tin with margarine and line the bottom with greaseproof paper.

2. Mix all the ingredients in a large mixing bowl and transfer to the cake tin. Level the surface.

3. Bake in the oven at 140°C (275°F, Gas Mark 1) for 2-2 ¼ hours. After 1 hour, cover the top of the cake with greaseproof paper to prevent the top becoming too brown.

4. The cake is cooked when the crust is firm to the touch and a skewer inserted into the middle of the cake comes out clean.

5. Let the cake cool in the tin before removing.

Honey Buns

Sweet treat

Stephen Fry is an English actor, screenwriter, author, playwright, journalist, poet, comedian, television presenter, film director and board member of Norwich City Football Club.

Stephen Fry was among the first to contribute to this book. Imagine our delight when we opened the post bag and found this waiting for us!

"Dear Karen, Vicki and Cath - Thank you very much for your letter requesting a recipe for this book you are compiling to raise money for Tŷ Hafan. I would like to contribute the following. Kind Regards, Stephen Fry"

Cooking time:
25 minutes

Makes:
1 batch

What you will need

2 eggs

75g (3 oz) caster sugar

1 tsp. soft dark brown sugar

Pinch of salt

90g (3 oz) self-raising flour

1 tsp. baking powder

90g (3 oz) butter, melted and cooled

1 tbsp. honey

How to make it

1. Whisk together the eggs and sugars.

2. Fold in the sifted flour, baking powder and salt.

3. Leave the mixture to rest for about 30 minutes.

4. Stir in the melted butter and honey.

5. Bake in cases for approx. 25 minutes at 180°C (350°F, Gas Mark 4).

© Claire Newman Williams

Lemon Drizzle Cake

Sweet treat

Kim works in our Procurement team as a Buyer, and is also a Foundations Committee member. Kim was on the cookbook editorial team, so it's thanks in part to her efforts that we have a book at all!

What more can I say than this is the cake I make on a regular basis for the guys in the office, my children love making it, and eating it with loads of custard, and it goes down a treat every time!

Cooking time:
1¾ hours

Makes:
20cm (8") cake

What you will need

225g (8 oz) butter, softened

225g (8 oz) caster sugar

4 lemons, zested then juiced

4 medium eggs

200g (7 oz) self-raising flour

1 tsp. baking powder

50g (2 oz) ground almonds

85g (3 oz) icing sugar

How to make it

1. Preheat the oven to 180°C (350°F, Gas Mark 4)

2. Grease and line the base of a 20cm (8") round cake tin

3. Mix the butter and caster sugar in a large bowl until pale and creamy.

4. Add the lemon zest and mix well. Add the eggs gradually, beating well with each addition.

5. Sift in the flour, baking powder and ground almonds and 4 tbsp. of the lemon juice and fold together until thoroughly combined.

6. Pour mixture into the prepared cake tin and bake for approximately 1 ¼ hours, or until a skewer inserted into the middle of the cake comes out clean. Leave to cool in the tin for 10 minutes.

7. Meanwhile, mix the icing sugar and the remaining lemon juice together to form a glaze.

8. Using a fork, prick holes in the top of the cake, and then pour the glaze evenly all over it.

9. Cool in the tin for a further 30 minutes, remove and serve – served best warm with lots of yummy custard!

Alan Thomas

Loaf Cake

Alan works as a Senior Estimator at Castleoak.

A recipe handed down to my wife, Brenda, by my mother, and baked to eat at many of our family/social gatherings.

Cooking time:
1 ½ - 1 ¾ hours

Makes:
1 loaf cake

What you will need

170g (6 oz) butter or margarine

170g (6 oz) caster sugar

225g (8 oz) self-raising flour

3 eggs

2 tbsp. milk

85g (3 oz) crushed walnuts, desiccated coconut or glacé cherries

How to make it

1. Grease and line a loaf tin.

2. Place all ingredients in a mixing bowl and beat with a wooden spoon until well mixed.

3. Transfer the mixture to the loaf tin.

4. Bake in the centre of the oven at 160°C (325°F, Gas Mark 3) for 1½-1¾ hours.

5. Leave to cool in the tin for 2-3 minutes, before removing from the tin and cooling on a wire cooling rack.

David Mahoney

Oreo Cheesecake

Dessert

David became a member of Only Men Aloud in 2009, after graduating from Oxford University where he studied music and was a choral scholar.

This was introduced to me by a fellow member of Only Men Aloud, and it's a bit of a guilty pleasure. I thoroughly recommend it!

Cooking time:
45 minutes

Makes:
12 servings

What you will need

24 Oreo Cookies, split into halves

3 tbsp. butter, melted

750g (26 ½ oz) cream cheese, softened

175g (6 oz) sugar

1 tsp. vanilla essence

3 eggs

How to make it

1. Preheat oven to 180°C (350°F, Gas Mark 4)

2. Place 16 of the cookies into a re-sealable plastic bag. Flatten the bag to remove excess air, then seal it. Finely crush the cookies by rolling a rolling pin over the bag repeatedly.

3. Place the crushed cookies in a mixing bowl. Add the butter; mix well. Press the mixture firmly into the bottom of a 23cm (9") springform pan to form the base.

4. Beat the cream cheese, sugar and vanilla essence in a large bowl with an electric mixer on medium speed until well blended. Add the eggs, one at a time, beating until just blended after each addition.

5. Chop or crush the remaining cookies. Gently stir half into the cream cheese mixture.

6. Pour the mixture over the prepared base; sprinkle with the remaining chopped cookies.

7. Bake for 45 minutes or until the centre is almost set. Remove from oven and allow to cool.

8. Refrigerate for 3 hours or overnight.

9. Cut into 12 portions and serve. Store leftover cheesecake in the fridge.

Celebrity contribution!

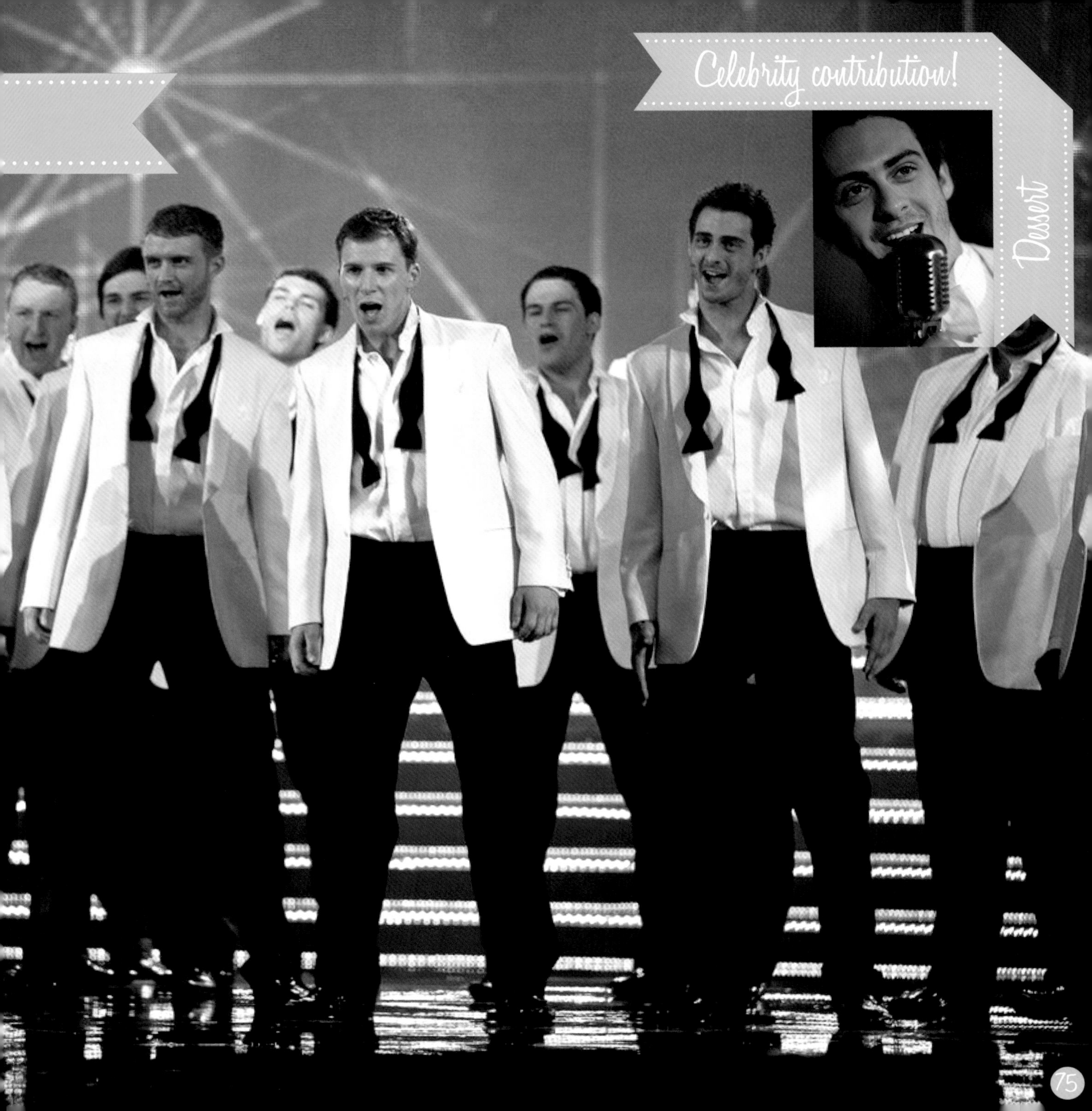

Karen Kennedy

Strawberry Shortcake

Karen is Castleoak's Projects Administrator and, when she's not doing that, she sits on the Foundations Committee.

This is a favourite recipe taken from my Mum's collection over the years.

Cooking time:
15 minutes

Makes:
18cm (7") cake

What you will need

200g (7 oz) self-raising flour

30g (1 oz) cornflour

Pinch of salt

85g (3 oz) butter

85g (3 oz) caster sugar

1 egg

6 tbsp. milk

140 ml (5 fl oz) cream, whipped

Strawberries or raspberries for decoration, halved

How to make it

1. Sift the flour, cornflour and salt into a mixing bowl.

2. Rub the butter into the flour with your fingertips until it resembles breadcrumbs and stir in 55g (2 oz) of the sugar.

3. Beat the egg with the milk and gradually add to the dry ingredients.

4. Turn the mixture onto a floured surface and knead for a few minutes until smooth.

5. Grease and flour two 18cm (7") cake tins. Divide the dough between the two tins, pressing into them lightly, and bake in the centre of a hot oven at 200°C (400°F, Gas Mark 6) for 15 minutes, or until golden. Turn the cakes onto a wire rack to cool.

6. Spread half of the whipped cream onto one of the cakes and decorate with the halved strawberries or raspberries. Dredge with a little sugar and top with the other cake.

7. Spread the remaining cream on top of the assembled cake and decorate with the rest of the fruit.

Graham Frost

Strawberry Swiss Roll

Graham is one of Castleoak's Construction Managers and spends most of his time on site, surrounded by scaffolding, overseeing the construction of our care homes.

This almost fat-free strawberry swiss roll recipe has all the taste of something more decadent but without any of the guilt! Feel free to vary the berries to suit your taste.

Cooking time:
15-20 minutes

Makes:
1 swiss roll

What you will need

1 250g (9 oz) tub of Quark cheese

4 eggs

5 tbsp. sweetener

1 tsp. vanilla essence

1 tsp. baking powder

6 strawberries, washed and sliced

How to make it

1. Separate the eggs.

2. With the yolks, mix in half of the quark, the baking powder, vanilla essence and 4 tbsp. of the sweetener.

3. Whisk half of the egg whites until thick and stiff. Stir into the yolk mix, before slowly stirring in the other half of the egg whites.

4. Spread out evenly into a non-stick baking tray and bake in the oven at 180°C (350°F, Gas Mark 4) for 15-20 minutes.

5. When cool, mix in the remaining sweetener with the rest of the quark cheese.

6. Spread this onto the cake, add the sliced strawberries, and roll from the short end to form a swiss roll.

 **Matt Tebbutt**

Teisen Lap

 *Sweet treat*

Celebrity chef and owner of the Foxhunter near Abergavenny

The Welsh cake, Teisen Lap, is a very traditional spiced, moist fruit cake baked in a shallow tray. This version uses the ancient recipe to create a delicious pudding.

Cooking time:
1 hour

Makes:
1 cake

What you will need

385g (13 ½ oz) caster sugar

385g (13 ½ oz) unsalted butter

385g (13 ½ oz) self-raising flour

3 generous tsp. mixed spice

300g (10 ½ oz) sultanas

Grated zest of 1 lemon and 1 orange

6 eggs, beaten

Welsh honey

Clotted cream

Sprigs of dried lavender

How to make it

1. Pre-soak the sultanas in freshly brewed tea and set aside.

2. Cream the butter and sugar until white and fluffy.

3. Whisk the eggs and very slowly add to the creamed butter and sugar, adding 1 tbsp. of the flour to prevent splitting.

4. Fold in the flour and mixed spice into the creamed mix.

5. Finally, fold in the drained sultanas, orange and lemon zest.

6. Transfer into greased and lined baking tray and bake in a pre-heated oven at 180°C (350°F, Gas Mark 4) for about 1 hour, or until a sharp knife inserted into the middle comes out clean.

7. Serve warm, with drizzles of honey and a dollop of clotted cream.

8. Decorate with sprigs of lavender.

Toffee

Sweet treat

Lydia works as an Administrator, ensuring the smooth running of Castleoak's in-house timber frame production factory in Ebbw Vale.

My Mam has made this every Halloween and Bonfire Night for as long as I can remember. She would make toffee apples and loose toffee for all the children that called to Trick or Treat, and hand it out by the bagful around the bonfire.

Even the grown ups would come looking for Mam's toffee.

My children have grown up with this tradition, just as I have, and we look forward to it every year. And every year she tells me that it's my turn to make it. Maybe this year I will have a go, under strict supervision of course.

Cooking time:
5-10 minutes

Makes:
1 batch

What you will need

450g (16 oz) brown sugar

40g (1 ½ oz) butter

2 tbsp. golden syrup

190 ml (6 ½ fl oz) water

1 tsp. vinegar

How to make it

1. Place all the ingredients in a saucepan and boil, stirring continuously. After about 5 minutes of boiling, use a spoon to take out some of the mixture and drop it into a bowl of cold water.

2. With your fingers, test the consistency. If the toffee is squidgy when pressed this will give a chewy texture. If you require a firmer toffee, boil for longer – the longer it's boiled for, the harder the toffee becomes. The mixture will snap upon testing when hard.

3. Pour the mixture into a baking tray or cake tin that has been lightly buttered.

4. Allow the toffee to cool before eating.

Elliot 19. 4. 12

biscuit the guinea

pigs

my Teddy sweets